Welcome to our sugar-free recipes for kids cookbook! As parents, we know that one of the biggest challenges is getting our children to eat healthy and nutritious meals. One of the biggest culprits in unhealthy diets is sugar. Kids love sugary treats, and it's easy to see why – sugar tastes great and is often used to make foods more appealing to little ones. However, consuming too much sugar can lead to a variety of health issues, such as obesity, diabetes, and tooth decay.

That's why we created this cookbook, filled with delicious and easy-to-make recipes that are completely sugar-free. We believe that healthy eating doesn't have to be boring, and that's why we've created a collection of recipes that are both nutritious and delicious. Our cookbook features a wide range of recipes, from breakfast ideas to snacks, lunch and dinner recipes, and even desserts, all made without any added sugars.

Our recipes are designed to be fun and appealing to kids, with bright colors, fun shapes, and tasty flavors that will keep them interested and excited about eating healthy food. We've included recipes that are easy enough for kids to help make, so they can get involved in the cooking process and learn about healthy eating habits.

We hope that this cookbook will be a valuable resource for parents looking for healthy and sugar-free meal ideas for their kids. We believe that by making healthy eating fun and accessible, we can help kids develop lifelong healthy eating habits that will benefit them for years to come. So, let's get cooking and enjoy some delicious and healthy meals together!

Protein Clinckers

INGREDIENTS

1 CUP (100G) CACAO POWDER, PLUS EXTRA TO COAT.
350G FIRM COCONUT OIL.
2 CUPS (500ML) RICE MALT SYRUP.
500G DESICCATED COCONUT.
100G VANILLA PROTEIN POWDER.
2 TSP EACH FINELY GRATED BEETROOT AND TURMERIC.
50G RASPBERRIES, FINELY CHOPPED.
FINELY GRATED ZEST AND JUICE OF 1 LEMON.

If you're looking for a delicious and healthy dessert with no added sugar, these sugar free protein clinckers are the perfect solution! They're simple to make, packed with nutritious ingredients, and taste amazing! Here's how to prepare them.

In a medium bowl mix together your cacao powder, coconut oil, rice malt syrup, desiccated coconut, protein powder, beetroot and turmeric. Add in the raspberries and lemon zest and juice, stirring until all ingredients are combined.

Using your hands or a spoon form the mixture into round balls about 2 inches in diameter. Place the balls on a tray lined with parchment paper and refrigerate for an hour or until set.

Once set, roll the balls in extra cacao powder, and store in an air tight container in the refrigerator. Enjoy your healthy and delicious sugar free protein clinckers with friends or family as a no-sugar dessert recipe! These are sure to be a hit at any gathering! Enjoy!

Chocolate Almond Cups

INGREDIENTS
1 HEAPING CUP VEGAN, REFINED SUGAR-FREE DARK CHOCOLATE
1 TABLESPOON COCONUT OIL.
½ CUP RAW CREAMY UNSALTED ALMOND BUTTER*
¼ CUP SUPERFINE BLANCHED ALMOND FLOUR.
2 TABLESPOON MAPLE SYRUP.
PINCH OF SALT.

Preparing these delicious Sugar Free Chocolate Almond Cups is a breeze. All you need to do is melt the vegan, refined sugar-free dark chocolate with the coconut oil, stirring until smooth and creamy. Then, spoon about 1 teaspoon of the melted chocolate into each cupcake liner. Top with a teaspoon of almond butter and sprinkle with almond flour. Repeat until all the cups are filled. Finally, drizzle each cup with a little of the maple syrup and sprinkle with a pinch of salt. Put in the refrigerator for at least 2 hours before serving.

These Sugar Free Chocolate Almond Cups make for a healthy dessert option that is no sugar but still just as delicious. They satisfy your sweet craving without compromising on flavor. With the simple ingredients and minimal preparation, you can whip these up in no time for an instant treat! Enjoy!

*Note: If you're using salted almond butter, don't add any more salt before baking. The extra salt won't be necessary. replace the almond butter with your favorite nut butter to make it your own. You can also switch up the dark chocolate for milk or white chocolate.

Chocolate Pudding

Sugar-free chocolate pudding is a healthy dessert option for those looking to enjoy sweet treats without compromising their health goals. With just five simple ingredients, this no-sugar dessert recipe can be easily prepared at home and enjoyed as a guilt-free treat.

To make this delicious sugar-free chocolate pudding, you will need heavy cream, unflavored gelatin powder, powdered erythritol, cocoa powder, sea salt and vanilla. Start by heating up the heavy cream in a saucepan until it is just under boiling point. Add the unflavored gelatin powder and let it simmer until it has dissolved. In a separate bowl, mix together the powdered erythritol and cocoa powder. Add this mixture to the heated cream, stirring until all of the ingredients are fully combined. Lastly, add a pinch of sea salt and some vanilla for flavor.

Let the mixture cool in the refrigerator for a few hours before serving your sugar-free chocolate pudding. Enjoy as is or top with fresh berries for an added burst of flavor. This delicious no-sugar dessert can be enjoyed any day of the week, so you can indulge without compromising your health goals!

Enjoy this easy and healthy sugar-free chocolate pudding recipe today!

Healthy Snickers

Making a healthy snickers bar is a great way to enjoy the classic treat without all of the added sugar. To make a delicious no-sugar dessert recipe, you will need medjool dates, peanut butter, nuts of your choice (almond, walnuts and peanuts work best), melted milk chocolate and coarse salt.

To prepare, first begin by pitting and chopping the dates. Then melt the milk chocolate in the microwave or over a double boiler. Next, combine chopped nuts of your choice with softened peanut butter and then mix in the chopped dates. Finally, spread this mixture onto a parchment paper-lined baking sheet and pour melted chocolate over it. Sprinkle with coarse salt and refrigerate until solid. You now have a delicious, no sugar dessert recipe that is sure to be a hit! Enjoy your healthy snickers bar!

Chocolate Avocado Mousse

Avocado and chocolate mousse is a delicious no sugar dessert recipe that is also healthy. To make this decadent treat, you will need two ripe avocados chopped, 200g of good quality dark eating chocolate (60-75% cocoa) broken into pieces, ½ cup of your preferred milk of choice such as cow's, almond or coconut milk, and two tablespoons of liquid honey or pure maple syrup (optional).

To prepare the mousse, first melt the chocolate in a heatproof bowl over simmering water or in a microwave. Once melted, set aside to cool slightly. In a food processor combine the avocados and stir with melted chocolate until combined and smooth. Add milk and sweetener of choice to the mixture and blend together until light and creamy.

Transfer the mousse into separate bowls or glasses, cover with cling film, and refrigerate for 1-2 hours. When ready to eat, enjoy - this delicious no sugar dessert recipe is guilt-free! Enjoy!

You can also serve the mousse with some fresh berries or grated dark chocolate for a touch of sweetness. No matter how you choose to enjoy your avocado and chocolate mousse, it definitely is a healthy dessert that will satisfy all taste buds! Enjoy!

Ricotta Cheesecake

Preparing sugar-free ricotta cheesecakes is an easy and healthy way to enjoy a delicious dessert without the added sugar. Here are the steps for how to make this no sugar dessert recipe:

1. In a large mixing bowl, combine 2 cups of ricotta cheese, 1/2 cup of sour cream, and 1/2 cup of stevia.

2. Add 1/4 teaspoon of lemon extract, along with 2 eggs and the grated zest from a lemon and orange.

3. Mix all ingredients together until you get a creamy texture. You can also add any extracts of your choice for additional flavorings, such as vanilla, almond, lemon or orange.

4. Grease a 9-inch cake pan with butter and pour the batter into it. Level the top of the batter using a spatula and bake in an oven preheated to 350°F for about 30 minutes. Insert a clean knife or toothpick in the center of the cake to check if it is ready.

5. Allow the cheesecake to cool for 15 minutes before serving. Enjoy your sugar-free ricotta cheesecake as a healthy dessert!

The result with be a delicious and healthy sugar-free treat that everyone can enjoy! Whether you are looking for no sugar dessert recipes or simply trying to cut down on the amount of sugar you consume, this recipe is a great way to satisfy your sweet tooth without the guilt. Enjoy!

Note: If you want to make mini cheesecakes, reduce the baking time by about 15 minutes and grease cupcake tins instead of one cake pan. The above ingredients are enough for 12

Pumpkin Pie

INGREDIENTS

1 (15-OUNCE) CAN PUMPKIN PUREE.
1 (12-OUNCE) CAN EVAPORATED MILK.
3 LARGE EGGS.
3/4 CUP GRANULATED ARTIFICIAL SWEETENER, SUCH AS SPLENDA OR TRUVIA.
1 TEASPOON GROUND CINNAMON.
1/2 TEASPOON GROUND GINGER.
1/4 TEASPOON GROUND NUTMEG.
1/4 TEASPOON SALT.

Pumpkin pie is a classic no sugar dessert recipe that can be enjoyed any time of the year. It's a healthy alternative to other high-sugar desserts, and it won't break the calorie bank. Preparing a pumpkin pie is easy with just a few simple steps.

First, preheat your oven to 350°F and grease a 9-inch pie pan.

In a large bowl, mix together 1 (15-ounce) can of pumpkin puree, 1 (12-ounce) can evaporated milk, 3 large eggs, 3/4 cup granulated artificial sweetener such as Splenda or Truvia, 1 teaspoon ground cinnamon, 1/2 teaspoon ground ginger, 1/4 teaspoon ground nutmeg, and 1/4 teaspoon salt. Whisk everything together until combined.

Pour the mixture into the prepared pie pan and bake for 50-55 minutes or until a knife inserted into the center of the pie comes out clean. Let cool before serving. Enjoy!

Straciatella Gelato

Making a sugar free stracciatella gelato is easy, and it's a great way to enjoy a no-sugar dessert. To prepare this healthy treat, you will need 585 g of whole milk with 3.5% fat, 200 g of cream with 30% fat, 105g Perfecto-X, 15 g Perfecto-Binder-X, 95 g xylitol, a pinch of salt, and optionally 10g Stracciatella ICE PASTE Movito and 5g Perfecto-Cremosa.

Start by combining the whole milk, cream, Perfecto-X, Perfecto-Binder-X, xylitol, and salt in a pot. Heat the ingredients over medium heat while stirring until they reach a temperature of 82°C (180°F). Then, remove the mixture from the heat and pour it into a bowl before letting it cool at room temperature. Once cooled, cover the bowl with plastic wrap and place it in the refrigerator for 3-4 hours.

Once the mixture has cooled and set, churn it in an ice cream maker according to the manufacturer's instructions. When the gelato is nearly finished churning, add in the Stracciatella ICE PASTE Movito and Perfecto-Cremosa (if using). Churn until thick and creamy then scoop into a container and freeze for 2-3 hours. Your sugar free stracciatella gelato is now ready to enjoy!

This delicious no-sugar dessert makes a great treat any time of year. Try experimenting with different flavors by adding in fresh fruits or other ingredients to create your own unique recipes. With just the right amount of sweetness, you can enjoy a guilt-free treat that's sure to satisfy your sweet tooth. Enjoy!

This recipe for sugar free stracciatella gelato is sure to become one of your favorite healthy dessert recipes. Delicious, creamy, and satisfying - what more could you want? Try it out today and see how easy it is to make a no-sugar dessert that everyone can enjoy. Enjoy!

Almond Banana Muffins

INGREDIENTS

BANANA MUFFINS ULTRA-FINE ALMOND FLOUR –
SALT
BAKING POWDER OR USE 1 TEASPOON OF BAKING SODA
INSTEAD.
CINNAMON
MASHED BANANAS – THE BEST ARE RIPE BANANAS TO
ADD LOTS OF BANANA FLAVOR AND AVOID ADDING ANY
SWEETENER IN THE RECIPE.
LARGE EGGS AT ROOM TEMPERATURE
COCONUT OIL OR MELTED BUTTER
VANILLA EXTRACT
STEVIA DROPS OR 1/3 CUP OF GRANULATED SWEETENER
OF CHOICE

These muffins are so good, you won't even miss the sugar! ripe bananas add natural sweetness and moisture, while almond flour and coconut oil keep them tender and rich.

To make them, simply combine all of the ingredients in a bowl and mix until well combined. Then, spoon the batter into a muffin tin and bake at 350 degrees F for about 20 minutes.

These almond banana muffins are a delicious and healthy dessert option - perfect for those looking for no sugar dessert recipes! If you want to add more sweetness, you can always drizzle with honey or maple syrup. Enjoy!

Brownies

INGREDIENTS

1 EGG.
1 EGG YOLK.
1/2 CUP AVOCADO OIL.
1/2 CUP TRUVIA *
1 TSP VANILLA.
1/3 CUP ALL PURPOSE FLOUR 48G.
1/3 CUP COCOA POWDER 27G.
1/4 TSP SALT.

Making sugar free brownies is a great way to enjoy a healthy dessert without any added sugar. Here's how you can make some delicious and nutritious brownies in no time!

To begin, preheat your oven to 350 degrees Fahrenheit. Then, whisk together the egg, egg yolk and avocado oil until light and fluffy. Next, mix in the Truvia, vanilla, flour, cocoa powder and salt.

Once everything is mixed together, pour the batter into a greased 8x8 baking dish. Bake for 20 minutes or until a toothpick inserted in the center comes out clean. Allow to cool completely before cutting into squares. Enjoy with your favorite no sugar dessert recipes!

Making sugar free brownies is a great way to enjoy a sweet treat without the added guilt. The combination of high-quality cocoa powder and Truvia makes for an irresistible dessert that will satisfy your cravings without any added sugar. Plus, it's easy to prepare and can be enjoyed with other healthy dessert recipes! So next time you are in the mood for something sweet, try making sugar free brownies!

You won't regret it. Enjoy!

Yogurt Sorbet

Yogurt sorbet is a refreshing, no-sugar dessert that provides a healthy alternative to sugary treats. It's easy to prepare and requires only three ingredients: Greek yogurt, granulated sweetener of choice, and optional vanilla extract.

To make this delicious treat you'll need to start by combining the Greek yogurt with the sweetener of your choice in a bowl. Stir until the sugar is completely dissolved. Then, add the vanilla extract and stir again to combine.

Once all the ingredients are mixed together, spoon the mixture into an ice cream maker and follow the manufacturer's instructions to churn it into a frozen sorbet. Alternatively, you can pour the mixture into a freezer-safe container and freeze it for several hours, stirring occasionally to break up any ice crystals that form.

When you're ready to serve the sorbet, scoop it into bowls or glasses and enjoy! Since there's no added sugar, this healthy dessert is perfect for anyone looking to satisfy their sweet tooth without consuming too many calories. And, it's sure to please everyone in the family - even the pickiest of eaters!

Chocolate Cookies

INGREDIENTS

1 CUP BUTTER, SOFTENED.
GRANULATED ERYTHRITOL EQUIVALENT
TO 1-1/2 CUPS GRANULATED SUGAR.
2 LARGE EGGS, ROOM TEMPERATURE.
1 TEASPOON VANILLA EXTRACT.
2-1/4 CUPS ALL-PURPOSE FLOUR.
1 TEASPOON BAKING SODA.
1 TEASPOON SALT.
2 CUPS SUGAR-FREE MILK CHOCOLATE
BAKING CHIPS.

Looking for a no sugar dessert recipe that is also healthy? Try making chocolate cookies with no added sugar. All you need are a few simple ingredients, including butter, granulated erythritol instead of sugar, eggs, vanilla extract, all-purpose flour, baking soda, salt and sugar-free milk chocolate baking chips. Here is how to prepare them:

1. Preheat oven to 375°F and line a baking sheet with parchment paper.

2. In bowl of electric mixer, cream the butter and erythritol on medium-high speed until light and fluffy. Add eggs one at a time, beating after each addition. Beat in the vanilla extract.

3. In a separate bowl, whisk together the flour, baking soda and salt; gradually add to butter mixture, scraping down sides of bowl as needed until combined. Stir in chocolate chips until evenly mixed throughout cookie batter.

4. Drop dough by rounded tablespoonfuls onto prepared baking sheet; bake 8 to 9 minutes, or until golden brown. Cool cookies completely before serving.

Enjoy a guilt-free dessert with these delicious no sugar chocolate cookies! They make the perfect healthy treat for any occasion. With simple ingredients and minimal effort, you can indulge in this sweet snack without sacrificing your health goals. Try out this recipe today and enjoy a tasty treat while sticking to your healthy diet.

Happy baking!

Raspberry Brownies

Ingredients

1/4 cup ground flaxseed.
3/4 cup water.
1 cup blanched almond flour.
3/4 cup cocoa powder.
1 teaspoon baking powder.
1/2 cup almond butter can sub for any nut or seed butter of choice.
1 teaspoon vanilla extract.
1/2 cup raspberries.

These raspberry brownies are a healthier and no-sugar alternative to traditional desserts. To prepare, start by preheating your oven to 350°F (176°C). In a small bowl, combine the ground flaxseed and water, stirring until well combined. Set aside for 10 minutes until thickened.

In a medium bowl, combine the almond flour, cocoa powder and baking powder. Add in the almond butter, vanilla extract, and flax egg mixture. Mix until well combined. Finally fold in the raspberries and stir them into your brownie batter.

Pour the batter into a greased 8x8 inch cake pan and bake for 30 minutes. Once done, remove the brownies from the oven and let cool before slicing and serving.

These raspberry brownies are a healthy, no-sugar alternative to traditional desserts. They can be enjoyed as an afternoon snack or for dessert after dinner. Enjoy!

Vanilla Muffins

INGREDIENTS

ALL PURPOSE FLOUR 1 ½ CUPS. ...
BAKING POWDER- 1 ½ TEASPOONS.
EGGS- 4.
SUGAR ALTERNATIVE- 1 ¾ CUPS EQUIVALENT TO SUGAR. ...
BUTTER- 1 ¾ STICKS (¾ CUP) MELTED.
VANILLA EXTRACT- 2 TEASPOONS.
MILK- ½ CUP AND ADDITIONAL (UP TO ¾ CUP TOTAL) IF BATTER SEEMS TOO THICK.

Vanilla muffins are a delicious and healthy dessert that can be easily prepared. With only a few ingredients, you can create a delightful no sugar treat. To start, preheat your oven to 350°F. Then in a bowl, mix together 1 ½ cups all-purpose flour and 1 ½ teaspoons baking powder. In another bowl, whisk together 4 eggs, 1 ¾ cups sugar alternative, and 1 ¾ sticks melted butter. Add 2 teaspoons vanilla extract to the egg mixture. Next, add the wet ingredients to the dry ingredients and mix until combined. If the batter seems too thick, you can add up to an additional ¾ cup of milk. Then pour the batter into a greased muffin tin and bake for 25-30 minutes. Enjoy your delicious and healthy no sugar dessert!

Protein Banana Bread

INGREDIENTS

2 MEDIUM BANANAS MASHED.
1 CUP MILK I USED UNSWEETENED ALMOND MILK.
1 TABLESPOON VINEGAR APPLE CIDER OR WHITE.
1 TEASPOON VANILLA EXTRACT.
2 CUPS SELF RISING FLOUR.
1/2 CUP ALMOND FLOUR.
1/4 CUP PROTEIN POWDER * SEE NOTES.
1/2 CUP BROWN SUGAR SUBSTITUTE OR ANY SWEETENER OF CHOICE.

Making healthy desserts isn't as hard as you think and with this no sugar banana bread recipe, it's easy to whip up a delicious snack in no time! To get started, preheat your oven to 350°F. In a large bowl, mash the two bananas until they are smooth. Then add the milk, vinegar, vanilla extract, self rising flour, almond flour, protein powder and sweetener of choice. Mix until all the ingredients are combined then pour into a prepared baking pan. Bake for 40 minutes or until a toothpick inserted in the center comes out clean. Allow to cool before serving. Enjoy!

This no sugar banana bread is perfect as part of your healthy dessert recipes repertoire. It's low in sugar, high in protein and a great way to satisfy your sweet tooth cravings. Plus, it takes only minutes to prepare and is totally worth the effort! So go ahead and give this delicious treat a try today. Bon appetit!

Strawberry Cheesecake Bars

INGREDIENTS

¾ CUP GRAHAM CRACKER CRUMBS. …
3 TABLESPOONS BUTTER, MELTED.
¼ TEASPOON GROUND CINNAMON.
¼ TEASPOON GROUND NUTMEG.
1 (8 OUNCE) PACKAGE CREAM CHEESE, SOFTENED.
1 ½ CUPS MILK.
1 (1 OUNCE) PACKAGE CHEESECAKE FLAVOR SUGAR-FREE INSTANT PUDDING MIX.
2 PINTS FRESH STRAWBERRIES, SLICED.

Strawberry cheesecake bars are a delicious and healthy dessert that won't add to your sugar intake. Preparing them is easy, and requires only a few simple steps:

1. Start by preheating the oven to 350 degrees Fahrenheit.

2. In a medium bowl, mix together the graham cracker crumbs, melted butter, cinnamon and nutmeg. Press the mixture into an 8x8 inch baking pan so that it forms an even layer on the bottom of the pan. Bake for 8 minutes, then let cool.

3. In a larger bowl, use an electric mixer to combine the cream cheese and milk until smooth and creamy. Beat in the pudding mix until completely blended.

4. Place the sliced strawberries on top of the graham cracker crust and pour the cream cheese mixture over it. Spread evenly with a spatula.

5. Bake for 25 minutes, then cool before cutting into bars and serving. Enjoy this delicious and healthy no-sugar dessert recipe!

With these simple steps, you can enjoy the delicious flavor of strawberry cheesecake bars without having to worry about how much sugar they contain. Try this recipe today and see how it satisfies your cravings for a sweet treat!

Ferrero Rocher Protein Balls

Ferrero Rocher Protein Balls are a delicious no-sugar dessert recipe that can be prepared in just minutes. Not only are these protein balls delicious, but they are also healthy for you too! The key ingredients for this tasty snack include protein powder, nut butter, cocoa powder (regular or dark), honey and chopped nuts.

If you're looking for a delicious and healthy dessert recipe, look no further than these ferrero rocher protein balls! Made with protein powder, nut butter, cocoa powder, honey, and chopped nuts, they're the perfect treat to satisfy your sweet tooth. And best of all, they're easy to make! Simply mix all of the ingredients together in a bowl and form into small balls. Place the balls on a cookie sheet lined with parchment paper, then bake at 350 F (177 C) for 10-15 minutes until golden brown. Let cool before serving and enjoy!

These protein balls are an excellent source of satiating protein, healthy fats, fiber, antioxidants, and vitamins and minerals. So not only do they taste great, but they're also good for you! Enjoy them as a post-workout snack or anytime you need a little energy boost.

Berry Pancakes

INGREDIENTS

1 CUP ALL PURPOSE FLOUR.
2 TABLESPOONS BUTTER.
1 TEASPOON BAKING POWDER.
1/4 CUP BLUE BERRIES.
1 CUP MILK.
1 EGG.
BUTTER OR OIL FOR FRYING.

Berry pancakes are an incredibly delicious and healthy no sugar dessert recipe that can be prepared in just a few simple steps. To make them, start by whisking together the all-purpose flour, baking powder and butter in a bowl. Then mix in the blueberries and milk until everything is fully combined. Next, crack one egg into the mixture to give it an extra boost of flavor and nutrition. Lastly, heat up a pan with some butter or oil before adding small scoops of the batter in to fry. Serve these yummy berry pancakes hot and enjoy as a healthy dessert!
The end result is sure to satisfy any sweet tooth without all the added sugar. You can even top them with a fresh fruit like strawberries or raspberries for extra sweetness. Enjoy!

Chocolate Chip Cookies

Making chocolate chip cookies is a fun and easy way to enjoy a no sugar dessert. To begin, preheat your oven to 375°F. Then prepare the ingredients: in a medium bowl, whisk together 2 cups of all-purpose flour, 1 teaspoon of baking soda and ½ teaspoon of salt; set aside. In another large bowl, mix 1 cup of softened butter and the sucralose-granulated sugar blend and sucralose-brown sugar blend together with an electric mixer until they are creamy. After that, add 2 teaspoons of vanilla extract and 2 eggs to the mixture. Beat until everything is combined. Gradually add the flour mixture to the wet ingredients and mix until everything is fully blended.

Finally, fold in your desired amount of chocolate chips into the dough. Drop spoonfuls of dough on an ungreased baking sheet and bake for 10-12 minutes or until golden brown. Let them cool before enjoying this healthy dessert! Enjoy your no sugar cookie masterpiece!

Chocolate Milkshake

A no sugar added chocolate milkshake is a healthy and delicious dessert that's easy to make. To create this treat, you'll need four scoops of no sugar added vanilla ice cream, 3/4 cup of whole milk, and 1oz of sugar free chocolate syrup. Here are the steps for how to prepare your no sugar added chocolate milkshake:

1. Place the four scoops of no sugar added vanilla ice cream in a blender and blend until it has a smooth consistency.
2. Add the 3/4 cup of whole milk to the mixture and blend until combined.
3. Add 1oz of sugar free chocolate syrup to the mixture and blend until incorporated.
4. Pour the milkshake into a glass and enjoy!

This no sugar added chocolate milkshake is perfect for those looking to indulge without the worry of excess sugar. It's also great for those who are trying to find healthy dessert recipes that still taste delicious. Enjoy your guilt-free treat!

Chocolate Avocado Truffles

INGREDIENTS

2/3 CUP MASHED AVOCADO (ABOUT 2 SMALL AVOCADOS)
1 1/2 CUPS LILY'S SUGAR FREE DARK CHOCOLATE CHIPS, DIVIDED.
1/2 TEASPOON VANILLA EXTRACT.
3 TABLESPOONS UNSWEETENED COCOA POWDER.
3 TABLESPOONS POWDERED MONK FRUIT.
1/4 CUP CHOPPED PEANUTS, OPTIONAL.
1 TEASPOON FLAKED SEA SALT, OPTIONAL.

Making chocolate avocado truffles is an easy and delicious way to enjoy a healthy no-sugar dessert. Here's how to make it:

1. In a medium bowl, mash 2 small avocados until smooth. Add 1 1/2 cups Lily's sugar free dark chocolate chips, 1/2 teaspoon of vanilla extract, 3 Tablespoons of unsweetened cocoa powder, and 3 Tablespoons of powdered monk fruit. Mix until everything is well combined.

2. Roll the mixture into 1-inch balls and place on a parchment paper-lined baking sheet. Place in the refrigerator for 10 minutes to let them set.

3. Remove from the refrigerator. Heat up the remaining 1/2 cup of chocolate chips in a double boiler or microwave until melted. Dip each truffle into the melted chocolate and place back on the baking sheet.

4. To finish, sprinkle with chopped peanuts, flaked sea salt, or another topping of your choice (optional). Let cool at room temperature for 10 minutes before serving. Enjoy!

These no-sugar chocolate avocado truffles are the perfect healthy dessert treat for any occasion. You can make them ahead of time and store in the refrigerator or freezer to have whenever a sweet craving hits. Give this easy recipe a try today!

Chocolate Mousse

INGREDIENTS

1 TABLESPOON COLD WATER.
1 TEASPOON UNFLAVORED GELATIN.
2 TABLESPOONS BOILING WATER.
1 CUP SPLENDA.
1/2 CUP UNSWEETENED COCOA POWDER, SUCH AS GHIRARDELLI.
1/8 TEASPOON SALT.
1 CUP HEAVY WHIPPING CREAM.
1 TEASPOON PURE VANILLA EXTRACT.

Chocolate mousse is a delicious no-sugar dessert recipe that is surprisingly healthy. It's easy to prepare and the perfect way to satisfy your sweet tooth without compromising your diet. To make it, start by combining one tablespoon of cold water with one teaspoon of unflavored gelatin in a small bowl. Then pour two tablespoons of boiling water over the top and stir until the gelatin has fully dissolved.

In a larger bowl, whisk together one cup of Splenda, 1/2 cup of unsweetened cocoa powder, and 1/8 teaspoon of salt. Slowly pour in the gelatin mixture while stirring continuously. Finally, add one cup of heavy whipping cream and one teaspoon of pure vanilla extract. Stir until everything is evenly combined and the mousse is smooth.

Refrigerate the mousse for at least two hours before serving. Enjoy!

Apple Muffins

INGREDIENTS

3/4 CUP WHOLE WHEAT FLOUR (OR
ALL-PURPOSE FLOUR IF PREFERRED)
1 TEASPOON BAKING POWDER.
1/8 TEASPOON SALT.
1/2 TEASPOON CINNAMON.
1/2 CUP BLUEBERRIES SMASHED.
1/2 CUP ALMOND MILK.
1 EGG.
1 TEASPOON VANILLA EXTRACT.

Now that you have your ingredients all ready, let's get to how to prepare these sugar free apple muffins. Start by preheating the oven to 375°F and lightly greasing a muffin tin with butter or nonstick cooking spray.

In a bowl, mix together the flour, baking powder, salt, and cinnamon. In another bowl, mix together the smashed blueberries, almond milk, egg, and vanilla extract. Add the wet ingredients to the dry ingredients and mix until everything is just combined.

Fill each muffin tin about three-quarters full with batter and bake for 15-18 minutes or until a toothpick or cake tester comes out clean. Let the muffins cool before serving.

These sugar free apple muffins make a healthy and delicious dessert that is perfect for any occasion. With no added sugar, you can indulge in a sweet treat without feeling guilty. Enjoy!

If you are looking for more ideas on how to enjoy healthy no-sugar desserts, then you should check out our other no-sugar dessert recipes on our blog. We have plenty of delicious ideas that are sure to satisfy your sweet tooth without all the sugar! Happy baking!

Have fun and enjoy! Healthy eating never tasted so good!

Vanilla Ice Cream

Vanilla ice cream is a classic treat that's enjoyed by both adults and kids alike. But how do you make it healthier? Here are some tips on how to prepare this no sugar dessert with just the right balance of flavor and nutrition.

First, choose an ice cream base that contains fewer added sugars like buttermilk, sorbitol, or maltitol. You can also look for one that's made with cream instead of milk to boost the fat content.

Next, add in some healthy ingredients like fresh fruit, nuts, or even protein powder to give your ice cream a nutritional boost. And lastly, don't forget to enjoy it in moderation! Just because it's healthier doesn't mean it's exempt from the usual rules of healthy eating.

With these tips in mind, you can easily make a delicious no-sugar dessert that can be enjoyed by everyone in your family. And for those days when you don't feel like making it yourself, there are plenty of store-bought ice cream brands that use healthy ingredients like whey protein concentrate, mono & diglycerides, guar gum, cellulose gum, and tara gum. So be sure to read the label before you buy!

By following these tips and making smart choices, you can enjoy a healthy dessert without all of the added sugars. With a few simple changes, vanilla ice cream can be a delicious and nutritious treat. Enjoy!

Apple Chips

If you're looking for a how to prepare no sugar dessert recipe that is both delicious and healthy, look no further than apple chips! The prep time is minimal, and the result is an irresistibly crunchy snack. To make apple chips, preheat your oven to 200°F. Thinly slice your apples, making sure to remove the seeds. Sprinkle them with cinnamon and bake for 1 hour, flipping the apples halfway through the baking time. Let your apple chips cool before indulging in this healthy dessert! Enjoy!

No matter how you choose to prepare your apples, there's no doubt that making a batch of crunchy apple chips is a great way to satisfy your sweet tooth without all the added sugar. With just a few simple ingredients and minimal prep time, you can make this delicious no-sugar dessert recipe in no time! Enjoy your crunchy, healthy snack today!

Sweet Potato Truffles

INGREDIENTS

1 ½ CUPS SWEET POTATO PUREE - 1 LARGE SWEET POTATO.
1 CUP ALMOND MEAL.
6 LARGE MEDJOOL DATES - PITTED AND SOAKED IN WARM WATER FOR 20 MINUTES.
3 TABLESPOON CACAO POWDER.
½ TEASPOON VANILLA.
1 CUP DESICCATED COCONUT - DIVIDED.

If you're looking for a healthy, no-sugar dessert recipe, these sweet potato truffles are a great option. They're easy to prepare and only require a few simple ingredients: sweet potato puree, almond meal, Medjool dates, cacao powder, vanilla, and desiccated coconut.

To make the truffles, start by preheating your oven to 375°F. Peel and cube one large sweet potato and place it in a baking dish. Bake for 30 minutes or until tender, then let cool and mash with a fork to make 1 ½ cups of sweet potato puree.

Next, soak 6 pitted Medjool dates in warm water for 20 minutes. Drain and add to a food processor along with 1 cup of almond meal, 3 tablespoons of cacao powder, ½ teaspoon of vanilla, and the sweet potato puree. Blend until smooth.

Line a baking sheet with parchment paper. Divide the mixture into 12 equal portions and use your hands to make small truffles. Roll each truffle in desiccated coconut until evenly coated, then place on the baking sheet.

Refrigerate for at least 2 hours before serving. Enjoy your delicious and healthy sweet potato truffles!

Low Carb Coconut Cookies

Ingredients
Coconut Flour- ⅓ cup.
Sugar free sweetener- 2 tablespoons. Use a liquid sweetener or a keto maple syrup.
Butter- ¼ cup, softened to room temperature.
Eggs- 2.
Optional ingredients add-ins such as shredded coconut, sugar free chocolate chips, or chopped nuts.

These low carb coconut cookies are the perfect no sugar dessert recipes that will satisfy any sweet tooth. They are easy to make and only require a few ingredients. Plus, they are healthy enough to be enjoyed as a snack or dessert.

To prepare these delicious treats, simply mix together the coconut flour, sugar free sweetener, softened butter, and eggs. Once the dough is formed, you can add in any optional ingredients of your choice such as shredded coconut, sugar free chocolate chips, or chopped nuts for more flavor and texture.

Once ready to bake, preheat the oven to 350F and line a cookie sheet with parchment paper. Using an ice cream scoop or two spoons, scoop out the dough and place them on the lined cookie sheet. Bake for 10-12 minutes or until golden brown and let cool completely before enjoying.

These low carb coconut cookies are a great healthy dessert to enjoy anytime! They have just enough sweetness without the guilt of unhealthy sugars so you can indulge in moderation. Enjoy these deliciously healthy treats with your family and friends.

Oatmeal Cookies

These no sugar oatmeal cookies are the perfect healthy dessert for any occasion. Whether you're looking for a sweet treat or just craving something delicious, these cookies won't disappoint.

To prepare this no-sugar dessert recipe, simply mix together two cups of rolled oats (like Great Value Old Fashioned Oats, 18 oz.), three mashed medium ripe bananas, a ½ cup of raisins (optional for those with a sweeter tooth), ⅓ cup applesauce, ¼ cup almond milk, one teaspoon vanilla extract, and one teaspoon ground cinnamon. Once all the ingredients are thoroughly combined, spoon the mixture onto an ungreased baking sheet and bake at 375 degrees Fahrenheit for 12-15 minutes.

When your no sugar oatmeal cookies are done baking, you'll be left with simple and delicious healthy dessert that everyone can enjoy. Enjoy this easy treat as is or with a scoop of your favorite ice cream for an extra sweet finish. No matter how you eat it, you'll be glad you made these no sugar oatmeal cookies. Enjoy!

Minicheesecakes

To prepare the delicious mini cheesecake bites, start by preheating your oven to 300°F. While it's heating up, you can begin making the crust. In a bowl, combine almond flour and melted butter until it forms a thick paste. Once that's ready, line a muffin tin with cupcake liners and press the crust into the bottoms. Then, bake for 15 minutes until it's lightly golden.

While that bakes, you can make the cheesecake filling. In a bowl, mix together cream cheese, powdered erythritol sweetener, eggs, vanilla extract and salt until smooth. Once your crust is done baking, carefully spoon the cheesecake filling into each cupcake liner. Bake for an additional 20 minutes until the tops are golden.

Let cool before serving and enjoy these healthy no sugar dessert recipes! Mini cheesecake bites make a great alternative to traditional sugary desserts so you can still satisfy your sweet tooth without compromising on nutrition. Enjoy!

I want to take a moment to express my heartfelt gratitude for your recent purchase of my recipe book. As a passionate food lover, nothing makes me happier than sharing my favorite recipes with others. Your decision to invest in my book not only supports my dream, but also shows your commitment to expanding your culinary horizons.

I sincerely hope that the recipes in the book will inspire you to try new things and add some excitement to your meals.

Thank you again for your support and for being a part of this journey with me. I hope my book will bring you many happy and delicious moments in the kitchen.